My God is Greater than Nine Centimeters

A Journey to Healing

H. L. Robertson

No part of this publication may be reproduced, stored in a retrieval system or transmitted in any way by any means, electronic, mechanical, photocopying, recording, or otherwise without the prior permission of the author except as provided by USA copyright law.

Scripture quotations are taken from the Holy Bible, King James Version, Cambridge, 1769. Used by permission. All rights reserved.

Book design copyright 2019 Fairhaven Media. All rights reserved.

Cover design by H L Robertson

Interior design by H L Robertson

Published in the United States of America

1. Religion/Biblical Criticism & Interpretation/General

2. Religion/Biblical Commentary/ General

16.03.31

ISBN: 978-1-947729-05-6

To all my brothers and sisters who stormed the gates of heaven on my behalf - prayer changes things!

&

Especially to my incredible wife and best friend who went unbelievably above and beyond to care for me during this trial; words fail me to express my gratitude and love.

Introduction

*I beseech you therefore, brethren, by the mercies of God,
that ye present your bodies a living sacrifice, holy,
acceptable unto God, which is your reasonable service.
And be not conformed to this world: but be ye transformed
by the renewing of your mind, that ye may prove what is
that good, and acceptable, and perfect, will of God.
Romans 12:1-2*

The passage above gives us an important framework for the interpretation of life's events. It tells us first that we need to 'present our bodies as a living sacrifice' so that we are submitted to God's will for us. It then proceeds to inform us quite bluntly that we are in need of a transformation from our native, worldly outlooks and thought processes to be conformed to the Lord's paradigms. This in turn allows us to be in a position to recognize and 'prove' what his will is and to follow it. The last phrases are telling: his will is good, acceptable, and perfect. The Greek word translated 'good' means that his will is beneficial to us. The next word, 'acceptable' means well-pleasing, so we can draw the conclusion that his will is both good for us and pleasing to him. The final word, 'perfect' is the Greek word 'telios' which confers a meaning of completeness and finality. This gives us a picture of the flow of events in our lives which in the past will appear as good and helpful, in the present are pleasing to God, and in the future will bring a completeness, fulfillment, and closure to our life's mission.

It's a rare occurrence that we encounter a situation or circumstance in our day to day existence that can truly be described as a 'life-change moment'; a point in time that is a defining moment. Even if we have such an occurrence we tend to gloss over it in the 'busyness' of life. Only from a safe distance in the downstream flow of life do we begin to understand the full impact and import of what has transpired. It has been said many times that hindsight is always 20-20. This is not always true but hindsight IS always hindsight. By this I mean that there is no guess work about what has actually happened in our life; at least if we're honest with ourselves. That fact, in and of itself, lends a significant amount of credibility to opinions and outlooks gained from the viewpoint of that 'down the road' perspective. We know what has happened but often fail to comprehend the why of what happened.

This is probably the single greatest obstacle to our recognition and comprehension of God's divine plans and purposes for us. Scripture tells us that he has these plans for our life but we all too often wander about oblivious to what they are and what they mean to us and for us. There seems to be a certain inevitability to the fact that we miss those significant events and moments. It is routinely discovered from the perspective of hindsight that what we perceived as ordinary, mundane situations and circumstances turn out to be the most earth-shaking junctures of our existence. Little do we realize at the time that something significant if happening. We have little or no inkling of the notion that something special and out of the ordinary is playing itself out in our lives; whether good or bad.

In this book I would like to tell you a story of one of those life-change moments in my life that I was incredibly blessed to recognize and appreciate as it played out. This wasn't a static point in time; it was an extended period in which some of the most profound encounters with the Lord I've ever experienced unfolded before me. I not only recognized them, but thankfully was given the faith and grace to embrace them and receive the fullness of what he was working in me and my life circumstances. This period of time, the events that it entailed, and the encounters with

God they produced, literally changed my life. My outlook on certain things was changed and my relationship with God was radically changed. It was a journey unlike anything I have ever experienced or even imagined. In these pages I will endeavor to allow you a glimpse into that journey and maybe even take you on a voyage through what those amazing weeks were like.

In Everything Give Thanks

In every thing give thanks: for this is the will of God in Christ Jesus concerning you. 1 Thess 5:18

Saturday January 27, 2018 – Back Injury

As I said in the introduction, it is so often the small occurrences, by all indications insignificant at the time, that can bring the most profound changes in our lives. Some of these things are incredibly good; some are devastatingly horrific. We just don't always know how they will turn out. Our earthbound, human view simply won't allow us to take in the whole panorama of God's plans and actions. That is why we have been given such a clear scriptural mandate to 'in every thing give thanks'. Notice that the verse says 'in' not 'for'. To be told to give thanks **for** something tends to lead us to believe that each and every scene that is played out in our existence is God's will and plan for us and therefore we must be thankful for it. Nothing could be further from the truth. The plain fact is that we live in a fallen, sin cursed world in which, frankly, the huge majority of what happens on a daily basis could in no way be said to be part of God's will and plan for humanity.

Sinful, dare I say evil, men and women carry out their lives operating solely from a Hedonistic, Humanist, Darwinist world view in which their success, advancement, and pleasure are the ultimate measuring sticks by which they judge what is good or bad. In this paradigm there is no absolute right or wrong. It is the individual person who decides how this is defined based on what are called situational ethics – if it's good for me it's good. If it hurts me it's bad. I realize this is broad brush look at the concept, but it is the core ideal of what that camp believes.

The Judeo-Christian paradigm paints a vastly different picture. The biblical worldview says that an omniscient, omnipotent God created all things, including mankind, for his will and pleasure; and therefore that creation belongs to him and is under his direction. His plans and purposes are paramount. All mankind's desires and wishes are subject to his ultimate authority. He has, however, given man a free will to choose his path and thus we have the dilemma of why evil exists in a world created and ruled over by a supreme being.

When I began this journey I was totally oblivious to the fact that I was in a 'game' of much higher stakes than I realized. Let me reiterate: the simplest actions and happenstances can have the most enormous consequences in our lives. In this case I simply hurt my back; or so I thought. While working on a small remodel my wife Sheila and I were doing on my mother-in-law's house I wrenched my lower spine. Was it good? No! I was in excruciating pain that had no let up. Over the counter pain medications barely touched it. By all humanist standards this was a terrifically negative accident. This injury, and a subsequent re-injury (yes, I hurt it twice) cost me a month of work, not to mention extensive pain and suffering. Please understand, I have worked in the construction industry most of my adult life and have had my share of minor to moderate injuries. This however was a totally different animal. The pain became so acute that by Sunday evening Sheila insisted I go to the emergency room.

While all this played out Sheila and I, along with a host of friends and relatives, were praying diligently for the pain to stop and my back to be healed. We were doing what we knew to do; bombard the throne of God with our petitions for what we assumed was the good and right thing to ask for. This is the point at which we reach the crux of the matter: we prayed for we thought was the best thing for me in this situation, but in reality it would have produced the worst possible outcome. Had those prayers been answered they would have brought about disastrous consequences for me. Once again we see as scriptures tell us "his ways are far above ours". His viewpoint from an eternal perspective is infinitely superior to our mortal, earth bound one. God sees 'the end from the beginning' we are told. We have no such luxury. We only see and comprehend the here-and-now. This viewpoint unfortunately leaves us ill-informed to make decisions about our situation and our future. This is why Jesus taught his disciples to pray: 'thy kingdom come, thy will be done'. He alone knows what the future holds and therefore is infinitely better qualified to direct our life choices.

Even the timing of the events was crucial to my well-being. If my trip to the ER had taken place on Saturday I perhaps would have received pain meds and anti-inflammatories before the suffering became so acute and I would have let the matter rest. However, by Sunday the situation became so bad that we, along with the medical staff, became concerned that I had possibly dislodged a kidney stone when I had the accident. This erroneous thought set into motion the whole chain of events that lead me to write this book.

The Discovery

Therefore judge nothing before the time, until the Lord come, who both will bring to light the hidden things of darkness… 1 Cor 4:5a

Sunday January 28th 2018 Tumor discovered in ER

As I wrote in the previous chapter this whole series of events began with an injury and was driven by the pain that resulted. The level of pain was unlike anything I've ever experienced. The ER personnel asked me what my pain level was on a scale of one-to-ten. My response was that a number of years ago I had accidentally shot myself in the hand with a pneumatic framing nailer and that I would gladly repeat that act if this pain would stop! Large doses of the most powerful pain medications available short of straight morphine were only moderately effective for short periods of time. I was given several massive doses of Toridol and Dilaudid before the pain became even temporarily manageable. I was then prescribed opioid pain medications that became the central focus of my existence for the next two weeks. It is very difficult to cope with life when you live it out in four hour increments; waiting for the next pain pill. I have never used recreational drugs, and have never in any way misused prescription drugs; this was a whole new world for me. I eventually discovered that simply by following my doctors' orders I had become mildly addicted to these meds and had the added layer of distress and pain in coming off of them. I ran a gauntlet of symptoms during the withdrawal process that only exacerbated the pain I was already enduring – another very negative experience.

The torment I was in caused Sheila and I to pray the previously mentioned prayers for pain to stop – we simply didn't know what we were asking God to do. James puts it this way:

Ye ask, and receive not, because ye ask amiss, that ye may consume it upon your lusts. James 4:3

This may seem like an odd verse to quote here but we have to remember that the word translated 'lust' here literally means pleasure and carries a connotation of desire. In accordance with what psychologists call the 'pleasure-pain principle' we will naturally seek what gives us pleasure and avoid what gives us pain. This is where we found ourselves. We were diligently seeking God asking for what would alleviate the pain. In this case we were praying what appeared to be a perfectly logical, common sense prayer when nothing could more dead wrong and if answered would have literally killed me! First Corinthians puts it this way:

For if I pray in an unknown tongue, my spirit prayeth, but my understanding is unfruitful. What is it then? I will pray with the spirit, and I will pray with the understanding also: I will sing with the spirit, and I will sing with the understanding also. 1 Cor 14:15

In this passage concerning the spiritual gift of praying in tongues the Apostle Paul gives us an interesting perspective on prayer. We are told to pray in the Spirit **and** pray with understanding. Regardless of your doctrinal thoughts or feelings about the spiritual gift, it is difficult to deny the applicability of Paul's admonition: there is a clear need to pray with understanding. In this case Sheila and I were sorely lacking in this important aspect of our petitions to God.

The area of concern was my lower back on the right side at my belt line. The fact that I had trace amounts of blood in my urine seemed to corroborate the notion that I had dislodged or aggravated a kidney stone when I wrenched my back. That is, after all, the general area in which one would expect to have pain with a kidney stone or stones. The level of pain I was enduring is also a common occurrence with that problem. Everything pointed to a stone as the culprit. It was such a seemingly clear cut diagnosis that the medical staff ordered a CT scan on my abdomen. I was prepped and transferred to a wheelchair and rolled through the hospital to the CT room. After the test I was wheeled back to my ER cubicle and waited as patiently as possible for the results. We were astounded when we were told that I didn't have a kidney stone but I **did** have a whopping nine centimeter (softball size) tumor on my left kidney.

While this came as quite a shock, we were calm during this time and had no fear. I felt sure that God would take care of this and simply prayed "Lord whatever gives you the greater glory we trust you to handle this however you want to. If you want to remove it supernaturally that's great. If you want to make it benign, that's great too. If you want a surgeon to remove it, that's OK too.' Finally! I was beginning to pray in the right way; or so I thought. I laid aside my thoughts and desires and let it rest in his hands to take care of in the best way; for me and for his glory. We now recognized that a positive answer to our previous, erroneous prayers could have possibly meant a death sentence for me. This was a sobering and humbling thought. How great is his love toward us that even in such a bad circumstance he does what is ultimately best for us; even when we are fervently praying for another outcome!

Peace That Passes All Understanding

And the peace of God, which passeth all understanding, shall keep your hearts and minds through Christ Jesus. Phil 4:7

MONDAY JANUARY 29TH 2018 Appointment with Dr. Tepedino - Urologist

TUESDAY JANUARY 30TH 2018 Appointment with Dr. Tucker – General Practitioner

From the very first instant in the ER that we were told about the tumor there was not a moment of fear; not one tear was shed; no worries erupted in our hearts and minds. There was only a 'flat line' emotionally. It was as if this was a non-event. We looked at each other and then looked at our pastor who was sitting with us in the ER cubicle. We both said 'it's Ok, God's got this', and that was that. It was a surreal experience. I have heard accounts my entire life of how people react when they hear the word 'tumor', or worse yet the 'C word'. There was simply none of that.

God supernaturally wrapped us in a spiritual blanket and gave us an inward knowing that he had this under control and this situation truly would be alright. We prayed together and I told the Lord it was his deal and left it in his hands. The peace we had was remarkable.

The hospital had arranged an appointment with Dr. Michael Tepedino who was the local urologist on call that night. On Monday we went to meet with him at his office. His immediate diagnosis was a clear cell/renal cell carcinoma. He told us that it wasn't a crisis and would be easily taken care of. He indicated that surgery would be required with the added comment that even if it was benign it would have to be removed because of its large size. He, without realizing it, underscored what a blessing we had received in this whole episode. His casual remark was: 'you hurting your back just saved your life'. He went on the tell us that this kind of tumor had no symptoms and that we would have never known it was there until it was too late to remedy the situation; adding 'when its softball size we can deal with it; when it's the size of a basketball there's nothing we can do'. He indicated that he could theoretically remove it but I would be much better off to have a specialist take it out lapariscopically. His office arranged an appointment with a surgeon at Vanderbilt Urology Clinic that specialized in this type of operation.

Personally, he gave me a prognosis of an 85% chance of coming out of this cancer free.

We also had an appointment at our general practitioner, Dr. Donald Tucker's office for Tuesday. We went to his office and conveyed what Dr. Tepedino had said. Dr. Tucker wasn't as casual in his outlook, being concerned about any chance of the malignancy spreading and wanted to see it dealt with, but still held a high probability that this would be fine. His attitude was: cancer is cancer. He was concerned but not overly worried. When asked about the surgeon we were scheduled to meet he responded: 'that's who I would want to go to'.

Once again the entire process was overshadowed by a profound sense of 'God's got this'. In fact, this became our regular answer to enquiries about my medical situation. It was a quiet assurance that the Lord was fully in control of the situation and everything was going to be alright. No worries clouded our outlook; there simply weren't any. Hebrews chapter 6 talks about this kind of hope and assurance:

Wherein God, willing more abundantly to shew unto the heirs of promise the immutability of his counsel, confirmed it by an oath: That by two immutable things, in which it was impossible for God to lie, we might have a strong consolation, who have fled for refuge to lay hold upon the hope set before us: Which hope we have as an anchor of the soul, both sure and stedfast, and which entereth into that within the veil…Heb 6:17-19

The Greek word translated 'consolation' is paraklesis from the same root word as parakletos which is the word translated 'comforter' referring to the Holy Spirit. One is the person of the Holy Spirit; the other is the action and activity of the Spirit. This was exactly what we were experiencing during this whole period of time encompassing the moment I hurt my back until it was all completed. In the passage Paul emphasizes the concept by using two different words to convey the same idea. First he uses the word 'sure' which indicates a certainty and a firmness in the promise we have been given. The second is 'stedfast' which indicates something unquestioned and immovable. This was the place we found ourselves in; covered by God's love and protection; and anchored in an immovable hope and assurance that he was sovereignly in control of this problem.

An Ark Prepared

But my God shall supply all your need according to his riches in glory by Christ Jesus. Phil 4:19

January 27th 2018 Back injury occurs

Entirely independent of my physical problems was a dilemma that threatened to swamp us before the surgery ever occurred. After my back was hurt I found myself unable to lie on my right side, lie on my back, or even sit up. My sacroiliac joint was severely sprained, pinching a nerve (the source of all the pain), and it took a significant amount of time to even begin to be noticeably better. I spent two weeks on opioid pain medications just to mediate some of the suffering. I was pretty much helpless during that time. After the initial two weeks were up I was able to sit up for short periods of time and lie on my back for brief periods. The thought of trying to work during the intervening time was an impossibility. We were facing a serious hit to our income. Our paint contracting business was doing well but we, as the only two employees, would simply have its manpower cut in half. The painting profession is a very physically demanding one. Not only that, but I couldn't drive while taking the pain medications.

During this time period we discovered that something remarkable was going on. Sheila was being supernaturally empowered to make money! Jobs that would normally have required both of us to work were now getting done in remarkably rapid fashion by her alone. In fact she was making as much money by herself as we normally made working together. It was as if God was giving her only jobs that could be done very quickly and incredibly profitably, but she was doing them with minimal amounts of stress and physical wear and tear. I felt guilty about her working alone while I slept most of the day, (the result of the pain meds) but when asked she would admit to being tired but not to the point she was breaking down in any way. It was amazing to sit back and watch what he was doing to meet our needs.

We discussed this and realized that once again God was honoring the tithes and offerings that we had made over the course of our marriage and was fulfilling his covenant promise to be Jehovah Jireh – the Lord our provider. In Malachi 4:10 he urges us to 'prove' him in our tithes and offerings and he will pour out a blessing we cannot contain. This is exactly what we were experiencing. The financial stream continued to flow in and every bill was paid and every need supplied. God empowered Sheila to accomplish tremendous things work-wise and then he added his blessing to the efforts being made. I have to take a moment here to say what an incredible job Sheila did during this time of balancing a very difficult work schedule, and at the same time caring for a near invalid husband. She was truly amazing and words would fail me to express my thankfulness for her. Just another tremendous blessing from above!

At the same time all this was happening I got another startling bit of news. An engineering job that had been on hold for nearly two months because of some ownership decisions that needed to be made suddenly got a go ahead. At the perfect moment when I was unable to participate in our primary business activities this opportunity to work on my part of this design project opened up. I was still limited in how long I could bear the pain of sitting up in a chair but I found I could sit at my computer CAD station for an hour or two, take a short break for a nap or just lie back in my recliner, and then resume my work. In this manner I was able to be productive during my downtime from our painting business. Once again God had orchestrated things to our greatest benefit at the time of our greatest need.

In another example of praying and desiring a particular outcome only to later find out just how misguided our thoughts were, we found that the delays in the pending engineering job I had been chafing at were actually benefitting us by the project proceeding just when I was unable to do any other productive work. In the end I wound up producing sixteen sheets of drawings during the time I was injured and unable to paint. God is so amazing! My complaints about the work schedule turned overnight into gratitude that I was able to complete my portion of the project at just the exact time for God to use that work as a bountiful blessing in our time of need.

When my surgery took place I was placed on a ten pound lifting restriction (strictly enforced by Sheila) for six weeks. Once again I was put in a position in which I couldn't work. First of all I was undergoing the healing process from a major surgery, but I was physically unable to work at our business. I was to be allowed to return to 'light duty', i.e. nothing physically stressful, and again within the lifting restriction, after approximately three and a half weeks. I was, however, warned by the surgeon that I would have little or no stamina for weeks to come. As before God worked things out so that just at the right time progress payments on the design job (the largest I've ever had) began to come in to supplement what Sheila was making in the painting business.

The whole episode of injuring my back most assuredly wasn't God's will, but he prepared the means to supply our needs and set them in motion before we even knew there was a need. His financial ark was already in place and ready before the whole sequence of events started. We came to realize that this was another reason why he had given us such incredible peace. He was able, from the viewpoint of eternity, to see the challenges coming in our lives and put in place the necessary measures to deal with them. As in the injury to my back, all our needs were met during the recovery from surgery and the following period even though I could do little or no productive work. All our needs were supplied without us missing a beat.

To show the abundance of his supply, by the time I was able to resume light duty work we were booked up for over two months in advance. I even received a job offer during the surgical downtime! It continues to amaze us going forward what unfathomable blessings we have been showered with.

Diagnosis

For ye are bought with a price: therefore glorify God in your body, and in your spirit, which are God's. 1 Cor 6:20

Tuesday February 6TH 2018 Needle biopsy – Dr. Tepedino

Friday February 9TH Pathology results – Dr. Tepedino

Monday March 19th 2018 – Dr. Smith – VMU Urology Clinic

At our initial visit to Dr. Tepedino's office he had his staff arrange an appointment with a surgeon, Dr. Joseph Smith at the Vanderbilt Medical Center Urology Clinic. Dr. Smith is a specialist in removing tumors of the kidney, bladder, prostate, etc. lapariscopically. As stated previously, Dr. Tepedino had recommended that the tumor be removed even if it was found to be benign. His prognosis was an 85% survival rate if it was, as he believed, clear cell carcinoma. He also was of the opinion that part, if not most, of the kidney could be saved and full function retained.

These were encouraging statements to say the least. We went home still feeling the assurance that God was handling this and everything would be fine.

The next day we got a call from Dr. Tepedino's office informing us that Dr. Smith had requested a needle biopsy be done. He was more comfortable dealing with this situation if he knew exactly what kind of tumor this was. Apparently he felt that this knowledge would affect how he approached the coming surgical procedure as to its type, scope, and duration. The procedure was scheduled for February 6th and we settled in for the week long wait.

At this juncture I was still holding onto the mindset of: "God is in control of this and however he chooses to handle it is fine with us." If the tumor was benign it still had to come out which meant surgery. If it was malignant it had to come out and so nothing changed. If it was supernaturally removed completely that was great but we left the situation in God's hands. After all, I **had** prayed "Lord however you want to handle this; whatever gives you the greater glory, that's what we want, and we leave it up to you." Now was the point in time at which this became a test of our commitment to that prayer. It would have been so very easy to get into fear and doubt, but the Holy Spirit continually gave us that peaceful reassurance that it was fine; that everything would turn out alright.

The day of the biopsy arrived and it was surreal in the total lack of emotion I felt. Sheila was calm but apprehensive for me; not about the procedure, but about how I felt about the procedure. Hers was the response of a loving, caring wife who would have rather had the needle stuck in her side than mine. Neither of us had any fears about the process of the biopsy itself. I was placed in a pre-op room, made to disrobe and put on one of those ridiculous hospital gowns. They then came and put in an IV butterfly into my arm and left me to wait for them to take me down to the room where they would perform the procedure. At the appointed time they came and gave me the first injection of what they referred to as "joy juice'. This is a pre-anesthesia cocktail of drugs that mellow you out to make you more relaxed while they begin their work. After my goodbyes to Sheila I was wheeled down to the CT scan room. Here I was made to lie on my stomach on the CT machine carriage. They then gave me another injection of an anesthetic drug and away I went! I remember nothing from that time until the procedure was completed and they were getting me back into the wheelchair to take me back to the pre-op room. I was informed all had gone perfectly and I was sent home.

On Friday February 9th we returned to Dr. Tepedino's office for the pathology results from the needle biopsy. He confirmed that it was malignant and that it was clear cell, also called renal cell, carcinoma. We now knew conclusively that it was malignant and that it definitely had to be removed. Again, there was no fear or negative emotion at this news; it was what it was but God was bigger! We were informed that now, armed with the confirmation of clear cell carcinoma, as opposed to possibly another, more aggressive type, that the prognosis was even better than the 85% rate we had been given earlier.

Our first appointment at the Vanderbilt Urology clinic was on Monday March 19th. The interview went very well. However, the surgeon wasn't as optimistic as Dr. Tepedino about the prognosis for the kidney. He was of the opinion that as far as the tumor had insinuated itself onto and into the kidney (nearly halfway) that it wasn't worth the risk of trying to save it on the chance that a rogue cell/s had escaped into the tissue that would be left. He said my other kidney was perfect and that I would never miss the one they were going to remove. In fact he made the astounding statement that I should have the surgery done and then go plan the rest of my life as if this had never happened! Dr Smith then referred me to a colleague of his, Dr Duke Harrell. Because of the size of the tumor he said this operation was more in line with Dr Harrell's subspecialty.

On March 20th we received a call from the Urology Clinic requesting that I have another CT scan done with and without the contrast dye, along with a chest x-ray. Dr. Smith wanted to confirm everything was in order before proceeding with the surgery. They gave me the option of having this done locally so as to avoid another trip to Nashville. After some confusion about how this would play out, I went to Dr. Tucker's office on March 22nd and the tests were performed. The office personnel tried to email the computer files from the tests and the reports to Vanderbilt but the files were too large and Vanderbilt needed a disk with them on it. I rushed the disk and report to them via Priority Mail. We later learned that part of those materials was misplaced and we ended up having to hand-carry a replacement set on the surgery day; but eventually everything got to the right place and we were left simply waiting for the surgery date to arrive.

Night Watches

Then spake the Lord to Paul in the night by a vision... Acts 18:9a

Saturday January 27th 2018 – injured my back

Sunday January 28th 2018 – in the emergency room

In the same way that God created a financial ark to prepare the means for us to survive financially far ahead of the need; he laid the groundwork for getting the two of us, especially me, to the place he needed us to be spiritually to be able to walk through this trial. At the same time that we were experiencing all the doctor's appointments and the diagnosis of cancer, we were dealing with a severe back injury that not only left me in excruciating pain for an extended period of time; but the life altering restrictions it placed on what I was and wasn't able to do. I couldn't work or even care for myself. I couldn't dress myself or put on shoes without help for several weeks.

In addition to being unable to work for most of the next month and a half, I was strictly limited, not by any doctor's restriction in my activities; but because of the pain. I couldn't sit upright, either in a chair or in bed. I couldn't lie or sleep on my back or my right side for three weeks. In fact, I spent so much time lying on my left side that I began to develop first abrasions and then calluses on my left elbow and ear. At the same time I was struggling with my eating habits. First, because I was unable to sit, I had to eat standing up. Sheila built a tall, chest high table for me out of scrap lumber (ironically from her mother's remodel job) so that I could use it to eat, watch TV, or simply stand leaning against it and rest. This 'tall table' was a staple in my life for almost a month.

The hardest thing to cope with was the recurring pain level spikes that rendered me essentially non-functional. I could only sleep for a couple of hours at a time before the pain drove me out of bed. I resorted to simply walking the floor waiting for the next pain pill. I was taking hydrocodone tablets (plus Finergren for the nausea I experienced from the pain medicine) like they were Tic-Tacs. I would get a period of relief from roughly an hour after taking my meds until about three hours after talking them. This means that roughly half of my existence during that period I was in a high level of pain. It is torturous to live your life in four hour increments waiting for the next dose of medication in hopes of getting some relief that all too often came briefly, sometimes not at all.

I spent weeks sleeping in brief snatches interspersed with what I refer to as my 'night watches'. These were many periods of time during the ramp up or fading away of the medication that I spent walking the balcony of our house in pain. These were in the dead of night when I could no longer stay in bed but would try not to wake Sheila. At the same time I was trying to move around in a mostly vain hope of finding a position or pattern of movement in which I got some ease from the agony I was going through. I began to find myself stopping, when the pain allowed, resting against the balcony handrail, gazing into the fireplace and reflecting on what was transpiring.

I grew in a way, to look forward to these times when I walked, prayed, cried, and talked to God. It was a period of the most profound closeness and intimacy with the Father that I've ever experienced. Scripture tells us to 'in all things give thanks'. I now comprehend that verse in a far deeper and richer way than I ever have before. I found myself truly thankful for those times of fellowship with God and the way they changed my outlook on so many areas of life. Even though I was dealing with pain on a level I had never encountered before, and added on top of that the prospects of undergoing a major, potentially life-altering surgery; I was blessed beyond measure for my nightly encounters with Father. This experience fundamentally changed my relationship with him. I reached a level of sweetness in our fellowship that I wouldn't trade for anything on earth.

In the end I began to fully understand the meaning of the old saying among Christians: " when all you have is God, you realize he's all you need".

A Word From the Lord

And the LORD came, and stood, and called as at other times, Samuel, Samuel. Then Samuel answered, Speak; for thy servant heareth. 1 Sam 3:10

Monday March 5, 2018 – Thursday March 8, 2108 Fresh Oil, New Wine conference

One critical juncture in this whole process was the period leading up to, and including, our long-planned trip to Hixson Tennessee for the Abba's House Church/Ron Phillips Ministries annual Fresh Oil – New Wine conference. This is an every year event for us and is a terrific time of spiritual refreshing and renewal. Taking place on March 5th-8th, this fell during a critical time between my diagnosis and the actual surgery. Sheila and I made a commitment to take communion together every day leading up to the conference. We were going to war for my health and recovery and sensed that the conference would be a watershed moment in this chain of events.

The opening service on Monday night was very uplifting but nothing 'out of the ordinary' occurred. The Tuesday morning session was a step-change up in intensity with incredible worship and ministry time. This ignited a sense of anticipation of more and better to come. We were not disappointed. The Tuesday night service began with an awesome worship time. During this time the worship atmosphere became almost overwhelming. I had an encounter with God during those moments unlike any but a rare and precious few that I have ever experienced. The physical, earthly environment around me seemed to fade and the rarified, heavenly atmosphere became more and more real until it seemed that all that existed at that moment was the Lord's presence and myself. It was wonderful beyond words. At that instant I heard in my spirit a message that wasn't audible but was more profound and tangible than spoken words. God said to me: "when all this is over and you come out on the other side, I want you to write about this journey you're on. That's your next book." I was stunned.

I then heard: "I want you to name it 'My God is bigger than nine centimeters'." The title I had been given had a sense of wonder about it; and yet was preposterous at the same time. The very idea that fallen flesh and medical science would try to pit something the size of a softball against the magnificence and power of the creator of the universe was almost comical to me. Every time I told someone the title God had given me I smiled and often laughed out loud. A sense of joy filled me at the thought of that name for the book. This was a point in time in which the Almighty was going to do something special and he had for some inexplicable reason chosen to do it for me!

I now felt an incredible sense of purpose and, dare I say, destiny. I had a direct mandate from God himself. This book is the fulfilling of that divine order. I had a mission, I had a title, and now it only remained for me to walk the rest of the path set before me and to write what I experienced. I didn't know or understand what all that would look like, but I knew beyond any doubt what I had to do. It also gave me a renewed sense of peace that God had a plan and purpose for me beyond that end-point of the process of surgery and recovery. I was told by well meaning friends at our church the Sunday following the conference that I couldn't 'leave' them. My response was: "I have a mandate from the Lord to write a book about all this. I'm not going anywhere".

Waiting

But they that wait upon the LORD shall renew their strength; they shall mount up with wings as eagles; they shall run, and not be weary; and they shall walk, and not faint. Isaiah 40:31

Monday March 26, 2018 Meeting with Dr Duke Ferrell, Vanderbilt University Medical Center

My initial meeting with Dr Ferrell went well. The surgery date was set for April 12th. Even though I had been waiting for what seemed an excruciatingly long time for my doctor's appointment, it was still to be seventeen days until my surgery – two and a half long weeks to twist in the wind. These two and a half weeks presented the perfect opportunity to let in worry and doubt; an open door for the situation and circumstances to undermine our faith. None of this happened though. The Lord provided the "peace that passes all understanding" so that there was no hint of faith wavering on my part or Sheila's. People asked repeatedly, in fact almost at every meeting, 'how do you feel'. My answer was an unfailing 'I feel great'. That was the part that seemed to mess people up: I was never sick! The doctors had told me from day one that there were no symptoms with this kind of cancer, and they were absolutely right. I had horrendous pain with my back injury, but not even a twinge from the kidney/tumor.

In a sense, the lack of symptoms made the waiting even more tedious. I wasn't in pain or suffering any side effects from it yet it seemed like a sort of internal 'sword of Damocles' hanging over me. When would I begin to have issues from it? Would they get it in time? What if symptoms began to appear? Again, the Lord kept my mind straight during this period; quietly reassuring me that it was going to be alright. My spirit man was at peace but my soulish part was antsy and just wanted it all over with. This was a tremendous object lesson in the principles of Romans 5:3 – 'tribulation worketh patience'.

During this period my back injury had healed to the extent that I could return to work. This was another strange aspect of the situation to reconcile in my mind. I had a monster inside my body that, if left untreated, could kill me; and yet, I was working every day. By all outward appearances and based simply on how I felt, I was seemingly in great shape. The fact that my back wasn't hurting or troubling me in any way was a huge relief. I was a walking time bomb but hadn't felt better in months. I now realize that God was giving me a window; a respite from the back issue for my body to gain strength for the surgery and recovery. I learned later from the doctors that they expected the healing process to take as long as a full year before I was back to full strength and stamina.

It was also during this waiting period that I learned the source of the tumor. I was told during one visit to the doctor's office for tests: 'this is an old person smoker's disease'. I replied that I had never smoked a single cigarette in my life. The inevitable follow up question was 'did your parents smoke?' I had to admit that yes my dad smoked the whole time I was growing up. I'm not playing the blame game here; it is simply a fact that second hand smoke can be deadly to those exposed to it. My dad, like millions of others during that era, had no idea that he was putting his family in jeopardy. I have since met with numerous individuals who have experienced the same result from second hand smoke – the same tumor on the same kidney resulting in the same surgery. Why it tends to be the left kidney is beyond me. Perhaps it is just one of those strange coincidences. Whatever the pathological, or moral and ethical implications, I was left to deal with the consequences.

About this same time period I was introduced to a series of teachings by Robert Henderson, a minister and Bible teacher. He has a series of books based on dealing with both physical and spiritual issues; especially attacks by satan based on the sins and iniquities of ourselves or our ancestors. This seemed a perfect opportunity to put those teachings into action. The process involves taking the enemy before God, the just judge, and asking for judgment against him for illegally and unjustly attacking us. We are God's children and have rights as such in His kingdom government and courts. I prayed through these issues and was once again assured by the Holy Spirit that all would be fine. I had now come to the place the Lord wanted me: I was, with the exception of the cursed tumor, sound in spirit, soul, and body and ready for what lay ahead.

Encounters

... who knoweth whether thou art come to the kingdom for such a time as this? Esther 4:14b

Thursday April 12th 2018 Surgical check in Vanderbilt University Medical Center

The day for my surgery finally arrived. All the waiting was over and it was time to get this thing taken care of. My part in the preparation was finished but God's wasn't as we would soon learn. I was due to arrive at 11:00 AM for a nominal noon surgery appointment. However, we got there early: 10:30, just to make sure there were no hitches in the process. On arrival in the surgical waiting area we registered at the main desk and were placed in queue for check-in. We were soon sent to a young woman in one of the check-in cubicles. Being our normal talkative selves, we soon learned that this young lady was a Christian and proceeded to talk with her about what was transpiring as we went through the check-in paperwork. This was a big encouragement that the Lord had just the right person waiting on us at this critical juncture. No cold, impersonal paper pushing bureaucrat; but a person who shared our faith that was a momentary bright spot in what could have been a very daunting day.

After check in we found seats in what was a typically crowded waiting area. We found ourselves sitting adjacent to two people from Kentucky who were there waiting for their loved one to return from surgery. Once again we struck up a conversation and found that the loved one in question was the lady's husband and the man's brother. And, by the way, he just happened to be a pastor. How great is God's love for us, to continually provide us with fellowship and encouragement from other believers when it is needed most!

Due to the normal stack up of many small incremental delays I wasn't taken out of the waiting area to the pre-op room until 12:30 with the surgery time pushed back to 1:30. Even in these last potentially tedious hours the Holy Spirit kept us calm and filled our hearts with peace. We simply weren't worried about the matter. The Lord had from the beginning set the tone for this whole process, starting with the lady at check-in and continuing throughout the whole day.

The Time Arrives

To every thing there is a season, and a time to every purpose under the heaven… a time to heal Eccl 3:1-3

Thursday April 12th 2018 Surgery Vanderbilt University Medical Center

As I said in the last chapter I was primed up and ready to go when I was taken to the pre-op room. Sheila and I had taken communion before we left home; calling into remembrance our covenant with Jehovah Rapha – the Lord who heals us. We had also prayed about the outcome and felt settled in our hearts that all would come out fine. Once again there were no nerves or worry. The sole moment of tension arose when it became clear that my wedding ring wouldn't come off. The anesthetist told me that he would have to cut it off because he didn't need to be amputating my finger if it swelled during the operation; he needed to be concentrating on putting me to sleep. After 35 years of marriage seeing my ring sawed off was a bitter blow but Sheila assured me we would get it repaired.

While the ring was being removed with a diamond saw a young woman walked up to the gurney and began talking to me about the tissue that was about to be removed. Catching her drift, I flatly replied: "you want my kidney and tumor." "Yes", she stated. I told her "When pathology is through with them you can have any or all of it. It's not like I'm going to put it on the mantle in a jar!" I then had to sign papers to that effect. I was also asked the first of seemingly an endless procession of times what I was being operated on for, and which side it was on. Apparently this is a failsafe to insure they got the correct kidney. All the while I was being rigged with monitor leads, an I.V. butterfly, etc.

As they prepared to take me to surgery I asked what I considered to be three all-important questions: was I going to be intubated, was I going to be catheterized, and especially, was I going to be awake for those procedures. I was told yes; both catheterization and intubation were going to take place, but was assured I would be out by then. This was a tremendous reassurance.

Just before they wheeled me to the O.R., Sheila and I hugged and kissed, as she reassured me repeatedly it was going to be alright. This sweet parting was the most difficult moment of the whole day. It was simply hard to let go in that moment. After we released our embrace they anesthetist gave me a shot of joy juice. I was still conscious but things were getting a little hazy.

I was rolled into the operating room and asked for the umpteenth time which side was being operated on. After all the paraphernalia was connected I was given another shot of joy juice and everything faded away.

Meanwhile, Sheila was being what she describes as a "pack mule"; carrying all our bags and gear by herself from the prep room back to the waiting room. Pastor Tim arrived at the waiting room late because of an automobile wreck - not his fault – and helped Sheila hold down the fort while I was in surgery. When time came to go to the recovery room he helped her be 'pack mule'.

All is Well

"It is well, it is well, with my soul…"

Hymn; Horatio Spafford

Thursday April 12th 2018 Recovery and Reunion

4 pm Friday April 13th Released

Monday April 16th First road trip for errands and out to lunch

Tuesday April 17th Itching all over

Wednesday April 18th Walked ½ mile

At approximately six PM, thirty minutes or so after the surgical team had finished closing me (with a combination of sutures and glue) I was moved to the recovery area. Sheila and Pastor Tim were allowed to come back to the recovery room even though I was still unconscious, but at least it was over! I was already there when they arrived, but still out of it. About an hour later I began to come to and process where I was and what had happened. The first thing I knew after I started coming to was Sheila talking to me. She told me the doctor said the operation went great and everything was fine. She then told me that Tim was there. Even at that point of half-stoned semi-consciousness my slightly warped gallows humor was in full force. I relied, "You say that like it's a good thing".

The next thing I became aware of as the sedation continued to wear off was that I was in a very significant amount of pain. Every time I moved in the bed, coughed, or even cleared my throat it was an adventure in pain. It felt like everything from my sternum to my pelvis had been ravaged by the surgeon. Once I saw under the bandages I realized that this was not really an exaggeration as I had an eight inch long incision along my belt line and four smaller holes for the laparoscopic instruments scattered around my abdomen.

At seven-thirty, about one hour after I woke up, I was wheeled to my hospital room with Sheila and Tim accompanying me. I don't remember much about the trip, but when we reached the room I was given the option of being lifted from the gurney to the bed or trying to walk on my own. For some unfathomable reason I heard myself say that I would walk. I very unsteadily got up (with the nurses' help) and walked the few steps to the bed. At this point in the process it felt like a major triumph, especially when it elicited a "you're a better man than I am, I'd be a wimp and make them carry me" quip from Tim.

Although I had been given pain meds I continued to have serious pain when I tried to make any kind of movement involving my abdominal muscles. I continued to doze for a short while until the nurse had me sit in the recliner by my bed. This was surprisingly easy and I soon found that it was less painful to move and shift my weight around in this upright position. Despite the pain the staff was very aggressive about my recovery and by midnight I was up making a very brief and unsteady walk down the hallway and back. This aggressive approach was carried on the next morning as the nurses again got me up into the recliner to sit while I had my breakfast. After roughly thirty-six hours of fasting I was ravenous; at this point I expected something like broth and Jell-o, but instead I received a full plate: eggs, toast, hash browns, oatmeal, fruit, juice, and coffee! I devoured it all and would have asked for seconds if that had been an option. Immediately after I had breakfast while Sheila had gone to eat hers, the nurse – a man thankfully – came in and removed my catheter. He then asked for a urine sample. Having just had my first fluids in a day and a half, I laughed in his face.

The walking regimen continued all day. By mid-afternoon I was able to a] produce a descent urine sample, and b] walk four laps around the urology nurses area. I also had several rounds of blood-work taken to insure my remaining kidney was functioning properly and all chemical and enzyme levels in my urine output were within acceptable ranges. They were; and consequently I was prepped for release. At four PM, approximately twenty-two hours after leaving the operating room I was released and wheeled to the sky bridge connecting to the parking garage. However, due to some strange quirk of hospital rules I had to walk from there to the truck on my own. Sheila drove back to Tullahoma to pick up my prescriptions while I posted selfies on Facebook. I felt a need to celebrate in some way!

Afterward

Being confident of this very thing, that he which hath begun a good work in you will perform it until the day of Jesus Christ: Phillipians 1:6

Saturday and Sunday I settled into a routine of eating, sleeping, sitting, and walking. I learned that the most significant pain associated with this type of surgery wasn't from the incisions or the internal procedures, although those certainly hurt, but instead arose from carbon dioxide that was trapped inside my body cavity. This gas is used to inflate the abdomen during the surgery to facilitate easier access to the organs. Unfortunately some gets trapped inside after the procedure is completed and the incisions sutured. This gas tends to migrate upward, putting pressure on the lungs, ribcage, and diaphragm causing horrible pain. The best and easiest, not to mention fastest, way to be rid of it is to walk. This promotes re-absorption of the CO_2 by the body, alleviating the pressure and thereby easing the pain. Needless to say, when I learned this I was highly motivated to speed the process by walking at every opportunity.

On Monday, just five days after the surgery, I had my first "road trip". Sheila took me with her to run some errands and then we went to our favorite Chinese restaurant for lunch.

Tuesday saw a new "complication" arise. The body hair on my chest and torso that had been shaved as I was prepped for surgery was beginning to grow back. This caused absolutely maddening itching all over the affected area with no way to scratch without causing an even worse discomfort by making contact with my incisions.

By Wednesday my daily walks were up to ½ mile each. I had moved from the house to the great outdoors to make laps around our shop building and eventually to the road and back. (Our driveway is 550' long!)

I settled into a routine for the next six weeks as I waited for my follow up appointment with the surgeon. At that point my exams, CT scan, and blood work all came back good and I was "released". I was scheduled for CT scans every six months for three years as a precaution. At this same time the surgeon went over the pathology reports with us and we learned that the cancer was completely contained inside the sack or "fascia" surrounding the kidney, and was confined to the kidney and tumor. There was another surprising fact we found out from the path report. We learned that God, in his faithfulness, had prepared me for this event from birth. The average adult male has kidneys that range from 10-13 centimeters in length. Mine were 19 centimeters! In a step reminiscent of Isaiah's prophecy that "…before they call, I will answer; and while they are yet speaking, I will hear." Isaiah 65:24. He had already provided the necessary capacity for my body to perform perfectly after the kidney was removed!

After I was released, and the ten pound lifting restriction removed, Sheila and I joined a gym, a pre-agreed upon step, in an attempt to get healthy and in better condition. However, I soon found the truth of the medical staff's admonition that it would take me a whole year to fully recover my strength and stamina.

I had a second follow up four months after I was released, including another CT scan to establish a new "baseline". Once again everything was perfectly normal and cancer-free. God is, and continues to be, very faithful.

Faux Pax

In the chapter entitled "Discovery" I record the following prayer: "Lord whatever gives you the greater glory we trust you to handle this however you want to. If you want to remove it supernaturally that's great. If you want to make it benign, that's great too. If you want a surgeon to remove it, that's OK too." I felt good about this prayer. After all, it was very sincere, it seemed altruistic, and was, to my way of thinking, submissive and humble. The only problem was that it was totally wrong! A few months after the surgery, I was studying some scriptural principles concerning divine healing for a message I was preparing. Little did I know that I was being "set up" by the Lord. One day as Sheila and I were discussing some ideas along the lines of God's desire and plan for healing (strictly in an abstract, theoretical vein; or so I thought) I was suddenly confronted very personally by the Lord regarding my own, very personal situation. After all, I am a staunch believer in divine healing; Sheila and I have both experienced it ourselves and have ministered healing to others. However in this situation, when I had a chance to stand in faith and receive a very important and necessary application of the covenant promise from "Jehovah Rapha", literally the Lord that heals (Exodus 15:26), I muffed it. The Lord was very firm about it. I prayed a very humble, spiritual sounding prayer that hadn't an ounce of faith in it! Instead of telling God what I needed and standing in faith in His covenant, I prayed a prayer that was faithless, opened the door for doubt, and killed any chance for healing; a triple threat!

I should have prayed a faith-filled prayer based on God's word:

Then they cry unto the Lord in their trouble, and he saveth them from their distresses. He sent his word and healed them, and delivered them from their destructions. Psalm 107:19-20

Here we see that his word is the answer to situations like this first and foremost. I have no issue with the medical profession. Some very highly skilled people literally saved my life. It is not; however, God's best for his people. In one of the greatest prophetic passages ever penned, Isaiah the "silver-tongued prophet" wrote:

...he was wounded for our transgressions, he was bruised for our iniquities; the chastisement of our peace was upon him; and with his stripes we are healed. Isaiah 53:5

It is obvious in this passage that healing was part of the atonement Jesus purchased through his suffering just the same as spiritual salvation and mental/emotional peace. Peter brings this concept forward into the New Covenant when he quotes this verse in 1 Peter 2:24 saying "we were healed". This divine healing is an accomplished fact settled on the cross. I simply failed to appropriate its virtue to myself by praying a tragically flawed prayer.

James 5 gives us a simple formula for approaching this type problem:

Is any sick among you? Let him call the elders of the church; and let them pray over him, anointing him with oil in the name of the Lord: And the prayer of faith shall save the sick, and the Lord shall raise him up… James 5:14-15

This was plainly a case in which I knew what to do, but failed to do it. James says that "faith without works is dead, being alone…" I had the faith and knowledge to see my situation resolved in a glorious manner, but missed my opportunity by uttering one faithless prayer. I have zero doubt that if I had prayed in the manner I should have I would be sitting here today with two healthy kidneys; and this book would be one chapter shorter. As I have reiterated many times; God is faithful. My story still has a happy ending, but the Lord didn't receive the glory for the miraculous intervention he would have if only I had cooperated. I hope this book encourages you and helps someone avoid the mistakes I made. To God be all glory!

The *Deep Wells Collection* is a compilation of six mini-books, previously published separately as Kindle e-books. These small, power packed books cover a wide variety of subjects ranging from the parable of the ten virgins to the symbolic meanings of wind in scripture to what Jesus wore when he was resurrected. Each book is full of scripture references and will stimulate the reader's curiosity to draw from the 'deep wells' of God's wisdom. Blessed are those who hunger and **thirst**...

Available on Amazon – ISBN 978-1-947729-01-8

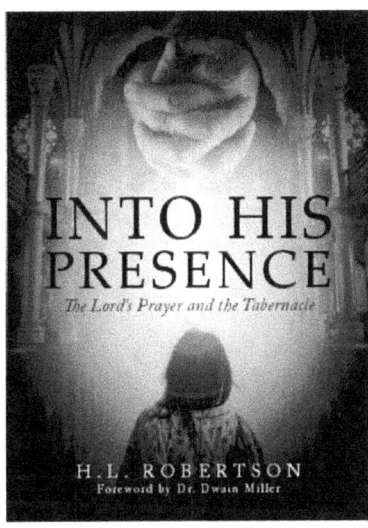

Into His Presence is a fresh and unique view of the Lord's Prayer. It is a phrase-by-phrase look at the most often repeated words ever spoken on this planet, combined with a step-by-step walk through of the Old Testament Tabernacle. Each phrase resonates with a part of the Old Testament worship process; showing that Jesus wasn't just teaching His followers a prayer to repeat, but that He was giving them a pathway to the intimate presence of His Father. His Jewish followers would have been closely acquainted with this type of worship, and as with so many of Jesus' teachings, would have understood these words on a far deeper level than most modern Christians would recognize. This book builds a framework of understanding for the reader, first of the Tabernacle worship system and then each phrase of the Lord's Prayer; explaining its meaning for us as believers and its significance in relation to the corresponding Tabernacle station. Also included in each chapter is a prayer of 'entering in' for that step in the journey.

Available on Amazon – ISBN 978-0-9987480-7-8

Sweet Aroma takes a unique viewpoint of the idea of our spiritual 'smell'. In this fascinating study, the author looks at the many scriptures dealing with this subject, including the aromas produced in the Tabernacle worship ceremonies, the stench of our fallen human nature in God's nostrils, and the extraordinary measures He took down through time to mask and cover our sin in order to pacify His holy anger toward us. Next, it investigates the concept of the blessing of the firstborn as first pictured in the story of Jacob and Esau; the role of Christ as the 'firstborn son', and the implications these principles have for us today. Finally it integrates these ideas into a framework for us to understand this revelation and to be able to proactively apply it to our everyday lives and our spiritual journey.

Available on Amazon – ISBN 978-0-9987480-6-1

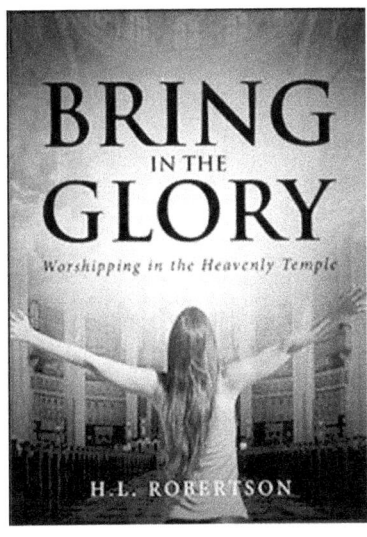

Have you ever tried to enter into worship only to 'hit a wall' and find you are unable to proceed deeper into God's presence and power? ***Bring in the Glory*** is an eye-opening look at both the worship process and the true dynamics of worship. It begins by establishing the concept of the heavenly temple and God's position in it. This is followed by an in depth study of the character and nature of worship in heaven; including its relationship to earthly worship, the role of the angels and the future role of the believers. It concludes with an examination of Davidic worship as a prophetic precursor to worship under the new covenant and the concept of pressing through the veil to bring the glory of God into our worship; both individually and corporately.

Available on Amazon – ISBN 978-0-9987480-8-5

Psalm 91 is perhaps the single most widely read, and quoted, scripture passage concerning divine protection. It is, in fact, 'stock in trade' for virtually any preacher, teacher, commentator, or writer dealing with the subject. It is also the best writing in scripture relating to the idea of a place of intimate fellowship and communion with God. Verses one and two in particular are not only quoted with great frequency, but are inscribed on plaques, bookmarks, Christian artwork, and other paraphernalia. This book examines this Psalm in detail along with Psalm 27, another very profound passage regarding this concept. It will also tie the 'secret place' David describes in the Psalms to other key concepts such as the tallit, the wedding canopy, Davidic worship, and Jesus' teachings on prayer.

Available on Amazon – ISBN 978-1-947729-01-8

Contact Information

You may contact the author or order additional copies at: hlrobertson.com.

To see the author's complete collection of printed books and Kindle books go to www.Amazon.com/author/hlrobertson

www.ingramcontent.com/pod-product-compliance
Lightning Source LLC
Chambersburg PA
CBHW050204130526
44591CB00034B/2096